Born-Child

poems by

Carol Anderheggen

Finishing Line Press
Georgetown, Kentucky

Born-Child

For Grace and Gram, my past
For Heather and Kate, my present
For Kylie and Cameron, my future

ACKNOWLEDGMENTS

My gratitude to the following regional publications which published these poems
for the first time:

A Letter among Friends: My Southern Heritage
Newport Life: Sin and Flesh Brook, Tiverton
The RI Writer's Circle Anthology 2010: Three Parents Down…
The Great Swamp Gazette: Mother's Day
NEARI Byline: An Uneasy Truce
Northeast Journal: Beached Upon Familiar Shores
NEARI Byline: A South County Vignette
Origami Poetry: A Little Love Poem
URI Women: Black on White

Publisher: Leah Maines

Editor: Christen Kincaid

Cover Art: Carol Anderheggen

Author Photo: Carol Anderheggen

Cover Design: Elizabeth Maines McCleavy

Printed in the USA on acid-free paper.
Order online: www.finishinglinepress.com
            also available on amazon.com

Author inquiries and mail orders:
Finishing Line Press
P. O. Box 1626
Georgetown, Kentucky 40324
U. S. A.

Table of Contents

Foreword

"The paradox is that people believe that "blood is thicker than water," and that a child always has ties and a sense of belonging to the family into which that child was born; however, they also believe that when a child is adopted, that child should 'belong' to the adoptive parents as much as any child belongs to parents who have given birth."

From *Adoption and the family system: strategies for treatment* by
Miriam Reitz and Kenneth Watson

Therein lies the paradox of the life I have lived and the source of most of the poetry I have written. In my adult life there are several persons who have been instrumental in teaching me how to be a human being despite those first twenty years.

So here begins the list of those persons and why:

> •Lenore, my Jewish mother, who had far more confidence in me as a young mother than I myself did;
> •Lynne, who taught me about "normal" family life by assuring me all things were not because I was adopted;
> •Peg, who taught me about sisters, and about constancy, and most of all about friendship;
> •Sandra, who reached into my darkness and pulled me out;
> •Warren, who helped me to believe that my poetry could be beautiful and truthful;
> •Shantia, the daughter who caused me to start the journey inward;
> •and Zoe, the daughter who tested my courage every step of the way.

These people form the touchstones of my fifty years as a grown child, otherwise known as an adult. Thanks also to Edit Kur for her experienced eye and ear for language and sound.

Passing the Torch

She swims, I'm told, every day,
her fetus cushioned in its own sea.
Her body, taut and agile,
like the eternal mermaid.

She beguiles with startling blue eyes
which drill deeply down,
down into the water of her being.

She gives birth—quickly,
almost easily—to a new one of her:
a little mermaid ready
to learn the siren's call
from the flesh of a master.

Transformation

Rising from the apparitions of night
I open the door to let the day in.
I yield only a tentative welcome,
as tentative as infant hands
seeking touch.

The dreams of night are still rehearsing
at my mind's backdoor, a shadow world
I've created and directed:
graceful dancers and strange animals
flying through the air, birch boughs
bending in the wind.

Soft light transforms the quiet morning air,
now crisp with a new day's expectations.
But I resist this beckoning from the safety of dreams
even as the soft light of sunrise seduces me,
finally softens me into day.

My Southern Heritage

The day my inheritors posed
small and southern
in front of the old car
whose weariness
was there revealed
still remains a secret:

> "See—in this picture of them
> standing by the car—
> clutching their dirty blankets—
> life's all pinched up in them."

Then, their scowls held vast meanings,
shining in their light blue eyes.
The missed lesson, the lost shoe,
scattered toys, dead goldfish,
now all of equal value—
leveled by memory
possessed only as reconstructed lives.

This visual reality,
this photographic reality
stares profoundly back at me
as my southern heritage,
glossed over by Yankee ice
still bursts forth
in those gray, scowling eyes.

Distance sweetens the loss
of daily parental privilege.
I survive remembering:
even this poem
had its transformations.

On Being Adopted

I have moved among many lives
here   there   elsewhere
a Navy captain and his wife
surviving Pearl Harbor
picking me up at an orphanage—
explaining mirages to me
as we sped along
a Florida state highway,
to meet my new grandmother.

The orphanage was no mirage.

She was busy at the sewing machine
making sun suits for her new and only
grandchild   me
what I knew of my foster mother
I bestowed on this sewing lady:
grey hair, blue eyes and the light
of liquid love in the eyes.

There was no liquid love otherwise.

Forget your first eight years
I was told.
Do not ask her questions,
buy a home, forswear the Navy life,
they were told.
Recipes for disaster doled out
by the well-intentioned.

Song of the Adopted Daughter

My two daddies were as different
as night and day:
one plebe, the other patrician
one with dancing blue eyes
the other steady brown
one fought to live, one lived to fight
one now dead, one lives still

        the sea, oh soft sea
          wash over me
        the sky, soft sky
          rise above me
        the leaves, soft leaves
          fall around me
        your eyes, your soft eyes
          settle upon me
        render me, render me
          your soft touch

In this they were alike:
each loving the same daughter
one fought for me, one fought with me
one mother found babbling
a year beyond my loss
the other, reluctant with envy
all the years of my presence

        the sea, the soft sea
          washes over me
        the sky, the soft sky
          rises above me
        the leaves, the soft leaves
          fall around me
        your eyes, your soft eyes
          settle upon me
        render me, render me
          your soft touch

Listen, my two daddies:
I am not now yours—
I never was—
Your time on me has run out,
the clock I am runs on

        render me, render me
          the sea, the sky, the leaves
        yes, render me
          your soft eyes, your soft touch

Sin and Flesh Brook, Tiverton

Dawn's pinks and greens
announce Easter Sunday.
The sun's centered stillness
glorifies bare branches
with a silvery silence
while lilies of the valley
surround a resurrection altar
of stones and tangles of roots.

Skippers gather sustenance
as the still chill air presses down
upon the lake, a mirror to the sky.
This Easter Sunday, two supplicants,
a father and a daughter,
steal away for trout fishing.
Their church is Sin and Flesh Brook
teeming with early morning life.

Father and daughter settle down
on their grassy pews, damp with dew,
quietly prepare to cast their lines
out onto the wide world of the pond.
While spiders scatter to salvage their webs,
and birds reassemble to observe
father and daughter worshipping,
Easter Sunday service thus begins.

Three parents down and one to go

I. My Prince Charming

Blazing blue eyes, that's how
I remember him: rugged,
a fighter who stole me away
from my first grade classroom.
What deadly calm came over us,
as he threatened our teacher
with a leafless stick—and I
excited and ashamed. More
ashamed of being excited
that my Prince Charming
had come at last, more
ashamed of that, than the deadly calm
and fear which rooted the class
to their safe little seats.

Only six, I, and with my Prince
Charming in my hand! We set sail
among palm trees, blue skies
and downtown Miami
in a junky automobile,
a Navaho blanket holding together
the tattered front seat.

The details of this particular excursion
blur into other rescues, other flights,
other fights...but always
the burly fighter-father
tenacious in the constant chaos
he created in my tender six year life.

II. She who bore me

Called me "her long-lost daughter"
with such a southern twang,
she already a stranger to me at five
when shown her picture—
I doubtful that I was
a born-child like others.

"Found in a box car a year after
the court took you," I was told.
"babbling in a box car," he said.
A sad end—or beginning—
for a Phi Beta Kappa
from the University of Tennessee.

This long lost daughter astonished
to find her alive, living like brother/
like sister with Prince Charming
in an old garage apartment.
As I balanced papaya juice
on my lap, she who bore me
asks politely if I'd had a good life.

III. The Captain

We had it out, not a few weeks
into our trial period as a family:
one pink sock, one white sock
satisfied my fledging fashion sense,
not so for the naval captain
who ordered otherwise.
One shoe flew at him and the other
at his demand for a matched set.

The corporeal punishment,
swiftly given, sealed his fate
with me. Never would or could
I be his emotional wife, though
he never stopped his pursuit
of owning my soul, a soul
a very stranger in its own body

We ended in a nursing home,
my reading weekly nature columns
to a father so incapacitated
by nature that he could not
speak, issue orders
or command his world naval-style.
He thanked me but never forgave

me my beloved, never forgave
the wife I had become,
just not to him.

IV. The One Left

I've loved the least, a true
wicked witch of the west,
now banana-curl clad
(weekly hair appointments
falling flat of beauty's goal.)
A spoiled porcelain mother-doll
the Iago of my adolescence.
She the daughter of a street peddler,
I (unbeknownst to me) a daughter
of southern educated aristocracy!

We've reached a detente,
this porcelain and I, a weekly
detente sweetened by candy
and powered by hearing aid batteries.
I throw her the lifeline of attention
she so deftly denied me.
These weekly visits are enough for me.
I'm learning more survival skills
than I'll ever need.

Mother's Day

Generations passing generations
a hallowed silence
as if we are
using words for the first time
connotations, denotations miss the mark
our silences growing louder
do we give what we want?
do we get what we need?

I bring you poems
you did not congratulate me
you did not rejoice in my good fortune
instead the Iago of your darkness
loomed—it is as it always was.
Your real self asserted herself
to announce how sorry
you were that I was not happy!

No no dear woman
whom I was forced to call mother all these years
no no dear frustrated woman
whom I was forced to kiss all these years
you knew me, you knew me well
that I could sing
that I could feel
that I could write and write it well.

I am your hope fulfilled
for which you have not the good sense
to admire, cheer on into life's pulsing crowd
I would it some other way
where light shines
into the tunnel shaft of our collective darkness
and we could love one another because we are alive
and not because we were forced upon one another
by time, circumstance and a man.

White Swans Rising

Arching already out-stretched necks
white swans rise, lift off mirrored water,
decision and motion as one.
One great flap of wings,
tips kissing the wet surface goodbye.
The air fills with their grace,
fills with white motion
as they undulate across the wide marsh
becoming specks in a sky
awash with the fading sunset.

In the marsh below white swans rising
fish undulate among the watery reeds
seeking sustenance in the murky waters
of this silken summer evening.
Near the marsh below, a lone child
chases fireflies while a dragon-fly
plays with the air, and the colors
of sunset yield to blue velvet night.

In her dreams the child rises,
touches the earth goodbye,
becomes a white swan rising,
filling the sky with the white motion of herself,
becomes a white swan rising,
flying away from watery grass, murky waters.

But here, on this earth, in this sky,
the stars go on like pinwheels,
silently spinning over the wide marsh,
over that one child with her fireflies,
alone—with her white swans rising.

Watcher in the Counting House

There stands at my mind's backdoor
a watcher: a stern figure
summing up my actions
a mathematical destination   a slate
of plusses and minuses with all
the eights written in reverse

maintaining a strong jaw line to hold
the ramparts   and keep silent
accounting of any relenting
that goes on (that is a minus)
unbemused eyes   sightless   colorless
calculate the next step
a divided brow   *tabula rasa*
records the concise calculations
storing all notations
on its brain's sheath

the watcher has heard tell
that the sum is greater
than its parts: since longing
is addition that terrible sum
of all that's gone before
and
all that's yet to come
the watcher does not move
off dead center
naught   zero   nothing
for terror is its own equilibrium
silent accounting its own pleasure
a balance sheet must balance
or

An Uneasy Truce

We slice off our lives
into little compartments
we call houses
and into corner rooms
place lamps
which shed pools of warm light,
on shells dragged
in from beachcombing;
shed light on photographs
of little boys in velveteen suits
(now become grandfathers),
on portraits of great grandmothers.

Into this dusky stillness
of rooms deserted by fly-away children,
only the competent tick
of a grandfather clock is heard.
The bright yellow-orange cat,
a newcomer to this domain,
licks her fur
unaware of ghosts of felines past,
of Easter egg hunts, Halloweens,
of the gathering of friends,
of safety from foes.

Into this space called home
crept loss—
its head dark,
its body a void.
Without invitation it settled
over desktops, over photographs
making of the stillness
an accusatory silence.

i fled its accusations
of actions taken and not taken,
i fled only to return
wiser and older
to fashion, without bravado,
an uneasy truce.

The Undertoad Is at Work Again

pulling me down
again
pulling me down
past the past
sabotaging the present
obscuring the future
leaving me in a present
where we all
forget about the myths,
the gods, the heroines
hiding in all of us

we live in the vacuum
of a bell jar
but some of us
wonder when or if
to come up for air
whether to open
that fragile window
so a kind apparition
might sneak in
to create a mischief
the undertoad
especially abhors

the undertoad knows,
knows that the goddesses,
gods and heroines lurk
waiting, waiting, waiting
to appear when time
and tide are right

(The author acknowledges her debt to John Irving for the word
undertoad.)

My Most Improbable Mother

Due to circumstances
beyond my control
life didn't deal me one
so I became the confused
infant I had once been
and again struggled
up to the light, up out of the darkness
that had been my friend, my pain,
my succor through the lean times

My most improbable mother
laid her slender hand
warm with life
on my breast lending me
her pulsations
so I could catch my breath
and believe for an instant
that there were no
wolves at my doorstep

My most improbable mother
cajoled me, challenged me
consoled me, cried for me
until I could cry for myself
heavy with realization
that the wolves lived
in my imagination
rich with promise

Due to circumstances
beyond my control
my most improbable mother
is now overwhelmed
with her own motherhood
rich with promise

I will cajole, challenge,
console, cry for her
until she can catch
her   breath

Beached upon Familiar Shores

This day will settle our griefs
with the cold punctuations
of brooding skies.
Our logic, our grammar
is spent.

The wild waves beat
their inexorable patterns
beyond our sentence
of time and space.

The little moonstones gleam
wet, so wet
as the reckless weather
shines
recessed in our eyes.

Gulls
grab the time
flinging it high
above us—
and we,
we are swept
as on the waves
seeking punctuations
in our lifetime.

A South County Vignette

A straight-down rain has glazed everything:
the gray barn siding of the backyard shed,
the white and purple lilacs lining my drive,
the maples, bereft of their broad green leaves,
rain glazed even my old Yankee neighbor,
a bent and wet protector to his geese.
Waiting for his arrival, they squawk
to the sky of the indignities
they suffer in service to humanity.
Dried feed corn, flung over their backs,
sinks into the little ponds.
It floats above the frozen ground
as pigeons dare the drawn rain
preparing to fight the geese
for the supremacy of the feed
and the Old Yankee shuffles away
oblivious

All My Edges Bristle

Perceptible movement has subtleties
that even the most perceptive of us
cannot grasp—
our minds defined by time and space,
our hearts disabled by patches of frost
across our trust—
though recognition flickers
in the eye of many
it blooms on the faces of a lucky few
who perhaps know not what they do.

Today my edges bristle—
silver gray trees, stripped,
make a farce of time.
I do not like it.
How can one, for instance,
know the real tree—
whether the green finery
of summer,
the sensual gray bark
of winter
or the magnificence
of fall-blaze?

All my edges bristle
the overflow of images
confounds me.
Which decade is alive?
The coquette
unaware of consequence,
the teacher
only taught, not teaching,
or the parent
sorely unparented?

Only the continuum exists after all.

A Little Love Poem

elbow to elbow, hand to hand
we accept our bodies' electric flow
illuminating our universe
for the moment—
now past consummation
we doze quietly
points touching
elbow to elbow, hand to hand

The Gift of the Cove

I. The Refuge

An untended shore, littered
with battered boats, castoff buoys,
netting of long-lost usefulness.
Haphazard seaweed decorations
cling securely
to the objects beneath,
saying the sea owns
all that is lost,
all that is abandoned.

Rotting seaweed scents this shore.

Despite the decay, the rot,
I hide here every spring afternoon
after school, away from martinis
and manhattans, hide amid
scattered empty beer bottles
and shells, empty of the lives
that made them.
An adolescent life,
as rife with loss as this beach,
with nothing to savor
or save.

II. The Beachcomber

At seven, my fair-haired daughter
became a beachcomber,
patient, sharp-eyed hunter,
hunched over, wresting
from sun-glittered sand
those small shards of pottery
and glass—green, blue, brown—
the precious, infrequent lavender.
I watch, unaffected by her
concentration, her joy.

Hauling her neon plastic pail home,
she washed her treasures

carefully, saving each one
hidden from my sight.
Now, in her tiny city apartment,
they nest in an old wooden bowl
shaped like the boats
once littering that shore.

III. The Return

The lights on the bridge,
like a double-stranded necklace,
seem to honor my return
to the pine-paneled cottage by the bay,
a home now that never was.
I explore the cove
though I need no refuge.
Someone cleaned it up—boats, buoys, nets
gone. As if someone rationalized it—
like a life finally understood.

No more seaweed rot scents the air.

My daughter invites me
into her private world of beachcombing.
Startled by her cove's beauty,
I let her teach me to be a beachcomber.

As gentle competitors we jostle,
shoulder to shoulder,
snatching what treasures the sand reveals.
Most highly prized, the broken pieces
of everyday china, with little flowers
and vines on them.

Back at the cottage, we compare,
trade pieces. We become intimates,
awash in the patina of the summer sunset.
Our angry passions no longer entwine, choking us.

This, a sufficient gift from a sufficient god.

This Marriage

admitted no impediments.
Nonetheless it sank
like a stone straight to the bottom
leaving behind ripples
of passion and indifference.

This marriage entwined us
in mutual fates of misapprehension
in dawns rising brilliantly
then sinking silently
into the recesses of our home.

Each little day, inexorable,
wound its light around
our family pictures, the warm stoves,
the marriage bed, crumpled and left
unmade.

Each child's footstep shuffled us
further away
into the child's life—into
our private sanctuaries
of convinced belief.

Yes. we sank. to the bottom.
inexorably down.
no more spirited hearts
willing to wrestle the world.
It was a death unlike any other.

It was a death like any other
as night dies with the sunrise
as one day dies for the next
as one child gives way for the next.

It was a death like and unlike any other.

Moonstone Beach

a place
where silence reigns
sky   sand   sea
a red-winged blackbird
fights the wind
perches precariously
on Christmas trees
denuded by Spring

a place
where self reigns
skin   sight   sensation
energy dancing
before my eye
pricks my surface
wafts me off center
into a greater silence

as huge
staccato waves beat
thick measures
sands smother
languid lovers
and over under all resounds
that mental undertow
     of seldom-seen friends
     of gay boys
     of children playing

echoes   echoes   echoes

November Rising

All the old losses reverberate
like bells rung out of tune:
dust beams through a rose window,
a black-robed choir braiding voices,
a flash of sun after dim light,
old faiths offering clarity
and constant revelation.

This new loss, Lady Retreat,
sits on her tombstone
before winter's death grip,
waving her long arms,
seeking a last minute remission—
though around her, green grass rising.

Maple leaves cede to the inevitable,
new palates of the October light
burnish the bushes,
new faiths of incredulous dying,
mutability and November rising.

What now do you mourn Lady Retreat?
Your futile gestures mime what regret?
Those eyes broad with grief,
those tiny hands gripping
that mossy-edged slab.

Watch out Lady Retreat!
Day's howling winds are at your back:
You grow small with grief,
smaller still your pride
and some say
you'll re-appear in the light
of a new and serious joy.

Black on White

Ravens on the ice pond today
pecked through snow
their beaks piercing
to the question
of food and winter survival.
I hurry to work on a road
ribboning its way
at the pond's edges
encasing the black and white
of ravens on snow.

        all that is winter
        seems colorless

I wonder at the winter survival
of ravens,
such blackness against opaque crystal,
of branches,
such gray longing against gray sky.
This is the time our futures
are frozen over
ice-locked
waiting.

Poems: a trilogy

i. preparing to leave

Into a sound white-washed room
drifts the scent of lemons
acrid, bitter, yellow,
surrounded by dark green leaves.
Only the azure sky breaks the monotony
of the brilliant white, brilliant walls
sealing me in—
only the azure sky with all its promise
mingles with the scent of lemons
in this room, this white-washed room.
When i leave this island
it will be
to travel back to civilization:
plumbing, fast food, hi-tech
only a jet-engine away.
When I travel back
it will be
to the miracle of personality
to the rise and fall
of too much, too fast.

if i leave this island.

ii. no safe harbors

there are no safe harbors
where water as pure as pure
where sky as clear as clear
exists:
in the mind where i exist
and seek such harbors

the little boats are joggled
by small waves
the stones at the shore
glisten with salt water,
the water's edge recedes
leaving behind starfish
seeking their refuge

among the wet stones.

there are no safe harbors—
the occasional storm
will whip its way through
upsetting in its path
a boat, a starfish, me.
Seaweed, churned, lands
at the tide's edge
tangled, indecipherable
glistening with the secrets
of a deep sea.

there are no safe harbors
only life rafts
here and there
spread across the landscape
of the sea
serving such purpose
as we can make of them

in the mind where i exist
and seek such harbors
the little boats are joggled
by small waves
and the stones at the shore
always glisten

iii. there is one joy

There is one joy: creation.
The stones, oh, the stones
turn into sands
into shorelines
the white-washed rooms
heavy with scent
split open
revealing the green-laden leaves
lush with azure-sky
and the promise of spring

There is one joy: re-creation.
When I leave it will be
to equilibrium, to a fine sense
of balance
between the white-washed room,
a coveted shoreline
and the fine stones.

I am here, I am here.

Practicing Migration

The field out back is dry and dead,
life's overhead
in a sky besotted
with the black punctuation marks
of birds: soaring, swooping,
then dividing:

they're practicing migration.

There were times when she wished
to escape: years ago,
when an urban forest of converging towers
rendered her anonymous,
a rock-solid void
then all she possessed.

She flew away nonetheless:
her young motherless arms
clutching her chicks,
her synapses short-circuiting,
creating palm trees, blue skies
out of place, out of time.

Birds steadily soar, swoop, divide:
born with instinct
to band together, head south or north,
depending on the planet's orbit,
depending on strength in unity.

Her mercurial mind
steered her south, an internal south:
alluring and warmer
than any New England winter
wrapping her in an illusion of safety,
a black unity of self.

She almost did not return.

Palm trees, blue skies appeared
cleansing her of city grime.
In this scene only pigeons

those dirty birds,
bag lady companions.
Pigeons, that admiring bog
of frenzied feeders,
con-birds, convincing
bag ladies they're not
alone.

She moved like a bag lady
in disguise—
a young mother, two children in tow.
Palm trees and blue skies
appeared and disappeared at will:
with no flock supporting her
her practice and flight were one.
It was a dreadful unity
from which she longed to return.

Now, every fall reminds her
she's learned to gather, to swoop,
to soar, then divide herself out,
to fly alone, settle on a high wire,
then drop in search of earth
toward that pine-paneled cottage by the bay,
where she's a migratory bird no more.

These Warm December Days

The blonde-headed girl walks barefoot
past children who hang pine wreaths
along an old clothesline—
two motorcyclists weave
through traffic—
such warmth as now envelops us
is rare—a December warmth
unheard of, not belonging
to our anticipations
of winter's howl
prowling around our hearts

Rare—these warm days—
rare in the long intervals of our lives
when nothing happens
when memories abound out of boredom
when faces have no finite distinctions—
but she—she walks in rare distinction
that blonde-headed girl:
her black shoes in hand,
her broad hips swaying her long skirt—
she marvels at these warm days
she is not frozen.

Transitions

I have leafed all morning
in this book of poetry
leaves falling endlessly falling

hieroglyphics written in 610 BC
by women endlessly longing
through the falling down centuries

this lake inside me is deep
threatens to overrun itself
but still remains unmoving

then seeps to the brim of longing
hovers to overflow to find
there are no more *what ifs* in my life

no dam will burst
in dizzying flood
careening into other lives

I am water
of ancient origins
liquid seeking my own level

a small motion could begin
at the very depth
smooth rhythmical swinging

of origins known
forgetting begetting
releasing reordering

reinstating the ancient
equilibrium
of a woman loving

The Child within Us

Touch earth:
And suppose you are a child again
Racing incessant waves
Against their own urgency.

Sense sky:
That bell-jar of infinity
Pressing down on the small figure
That is you staring back
Into your own blue infinity.

Taste salt:
Of Atlantic seawater, of bristling tears
Turning into brine, as Time dwells
Incessantly in the shell of your sensation.

Take time:
(An artificial distinction between then and now)
And press it close, salt away pain,
Fling it high above you, crack the glass,
Then, only then,

Touch earth.

Though born **Carol Mae Ray** in Miami, Florida, and, though I still love the sight of green fronds waving in a breeze against an azure sky, I am a transplanted New Englander now. I live a busy retired life in Rhode Island under the name Carol Anderheggen. In addition to writing (and being published in regional journals here in the Northeast) I am an active American Red Cross volunteer.

My spiritual home for my poetic self was The Frost Place, Franconia, NH where I worked on the staff of The Frost Festival of Poetry for many summers. Now, as an active poet in the Northeast I am much privileged to be a part of the Ocean State Poets whose mission it is to bring the joy of poetry to unserved and underserved venues in Rhode Island. I have set up our OSP website (www.oceanstatepoets.org) and also my own website (www.carolmaeray.com).

Along with another poet I assisted in running a monthly workshop on poetry at a local public library. We met for over two years and have appeared in two local publications, *The Bay* and *Newport Life*. Working with the same poet I facilitate a poetry workshop at Salve Regina University in Newport, RI which involves both developmentally disabled adults from the community and Salve students. This program has been running for over five years.

My first chapbook, *Writing Down Cancer*, was published in 2015 by Finishing Line Press. Publications which have published my poetry include *Newport Life, A Letter Among Friends, NEARI Bylines, Hope Center for Cancer Support, RI Breast Cancer Coalition, Northeast Journal, Anemone, URI Women, The Great Swamp Gazette.*

www.ingramcontent.com/pod-product-compliance
Lightning Source LLC
LaVergne TN
LVHW051608080426
835510LV00020B/3190